The Art of Decorative Paper Stencils 2

QUARRY

BEVERLY MASSACHUSETTS

TRAVELING WITH STENCILS

THE ART OF DECORATIVE PAPER STENCILS 2

KANAKO YAGUCHI

QUARRY BOOKS

First published in 2007 in Japan by
Ikeda Shoten Publishing Co. Ltd.,
43 Benten-cho, Shinjuku-ku, Tokyo 162-0851, Japan
www.ikedashoten.co.jp
under the title of *Yasashii Kirigami 2*

First published in 2009 in the United States of America by
Quarry Books, a member of
Quayside Publishing Group
100 Cummings Center / 406-L
Beverly, Massachusetts 01915
USA
Phone: 978-282-9590
FAX: 978-283-2742
www.rockpub.com

English translation rights arranged with
Ikeda Shoten Publishing co., LTD
through Rico Komanoya, ricorico, Tokyo, Japan.

Translation: Seishi Maruyama
Copy-editing: Alma R. H. Reyes
Editing: Omegasha Co., Ltd.
Art direction: Takuji Segawa (Killigraph)
Book Design: Eiko Nishida (cooltiger, ltd.) and
Andrew Pothecary (forbiddencolour)
Photographs: Kazutoshi Watanabe, Tomohiro Akasaka
Photo Collaboration: Found and biotope (for the cabinets
and tables on pages 80 to 93)
Illustration: Kiiyoshi Matsui
Production: Aki Ueda (ricorico)
Chief editor and producer: Rico Komanoya (ricorico)

ISBN-13: 978-1-59253-538-5
ISBN-10: 1-59253-538-0

10 9 8 7 6 5 4 3 2 1

Printed in China by Everbest Printing Co., Ltd.

Contents

World Travel Memoir with Paper Stencils

In this book I would like to narrate the stories of my travels with my scissors and paper at hand. I'm sure that everyone has had at least some experience with paper cutting as a child. Paper handicraft may look familiar, but it can also offer new ideas. You cannot make the exact same shape twice, which makes this artwork fun.

Traveling has the same concept. Every trip may not always be smooth, but a little bit of adventure and failure along the way can add spice to your experience. I always cut paper as if I was carving memories from my travels. Sometimes I cut too much, and other times I want to take a break, but I always encounter something new during the process. Just imagine that the paper stencils take you to all the cities around the world, as though you were walking and looking around in a foreign town.

I hope these decorative paper stencils can successfully narrate my travel memories.

Kamakura, Japan

The midday sun shines intensely in summer. I feel the breeze while walking slowly along the beach. I can smell the air at night, which reminds me of something in my past. The fragrance of coffee from a café in the back alley is bitter and nostalgic. I take a short trip to the suburbs.

San Francisco, U.S.A.

Gradations of light and dark green sway against the small apartment windows. Other various colors scatter around the city. The scent of young leaves reminds me of different scenes from my precious memories.

Montego Bay, Jamaica

Flowers bloom all over
the landscape, just like in
a scene I dreamt of one day.
Sunshine glows everywhere
on this hot island. Colorful
cold drinks taste so sweet,
mellow, and magical. I stroll
along the beach at dusk
while following the smells
of exotic fruits.

Prague, Czech Republic ▶

There are many mysterious
legends and fairy tales about
this city that people dream
about. They keep their
traditions, yet never cease
to create new things. I walk
cheerfully on the streets,
through the crowd of happy
locals while following
their footsteps.

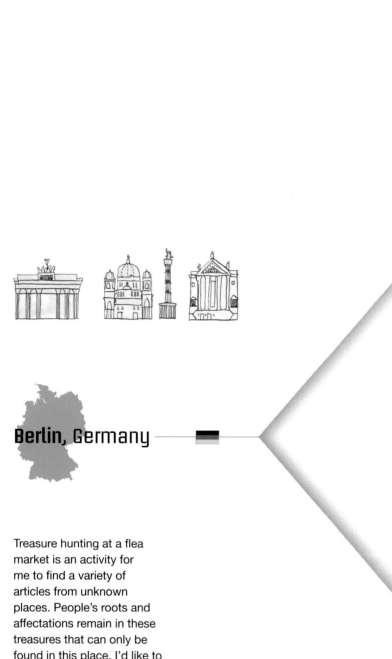

Berlin, Germany

Treasure hunting at a flea market is an activity for me to find a variety of articles from unknown places. People's roots and affectations remain in these treasures that can only be found in this place. I'd like to leave my sentiments in this city and look forward to my next visit someday.

Vienna, Austria

I walk on a long, straight path toward the magnificent palace amidst a clear and cold air. Guided by the museum's particular scent, I walk toward the drawing on its front façade. As I pause, the landscape of the olden days unfolds before my eyes.

How to Use This Book

You can create decorative paper stencils in three easy steps: fold, cut, and open. First, choose the paper for the design that you want to make. Then, choose one of the three basic folding patterns. When you have finished folding a basic pattern, draw the pattern, place the folded paper on the same side as the drawn pattern, and cut the paper while leaving the colored parts.

This book also explains the procedures and methods of cutting a stencil for each pattern. However, the designs introduced in this book are only for reference. You can find your own comfortable way of making decorative paper stencils.

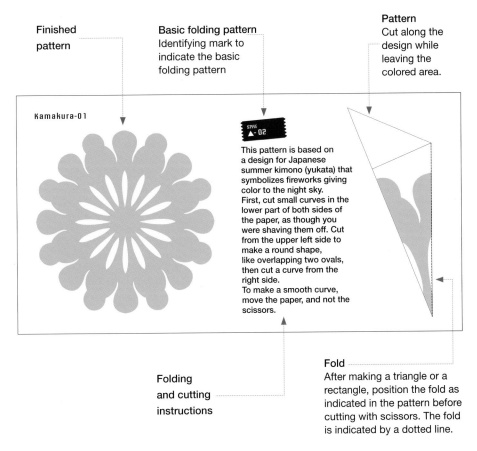

Finished pattern

Basic folding pattern
Identifying mark to indicate the basic folding pattern

Pattern
Cut along the design while leaving the colored area.

Kamakura-01

STYLE
▲- 02

This pattern is based on a design for Japanese summer kimono (yukata) that symbolizes fireworks giving color to the night sky.
First, cut small curves in the lower part of both sides of the paper, as though you were shaving them off. Cut from the upper left side to make a round shape, like overlapping two ovals, then cut a curve from the right side.
To make a smooth curve, move the paper, and not the scissors.

Folding and cutting instructions

Fold
After making a triangle or a rectangle, position the fold as indicated in the pattern before cutting with scissors. The fold is indicated by a dotted line.

Scissors
One of the necessary tools that you need to prepare for paper-stencil making is a pair of scissors. Select one that fits comfortably in your hand.

Paper (origami paper)
You can use any type of colored paper, but origami paper is preferable and is readily available. It should not be too thick and can come in any size, so you can cut a small sheet into a square.

Glue
You need glue to stick your finished work on a sketchbook. You can use a glue stick, spray glue, or liquid glue depending on the type of paper you are using.

Sketchbook
You can keep origami paper, business cards and newspapers you have collected on your trips, and many other types of paper in a sketchbook. This will serve as your travel book.

Basic folding Patterns

Paper stencils are very simple to create. All you have to do is fold, cut, and open. You don't have to limit yourself to origami paper; you can also use other types of paper that you collect from various places you have travelled. What shape would you like to cut?

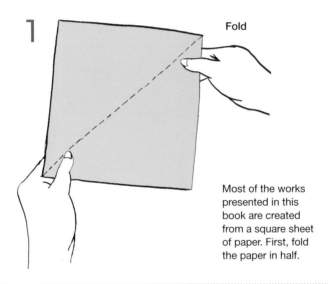

1 Fold

Most of the works presented in this book are created from a square sheet of paper. First, fold the paper in half.

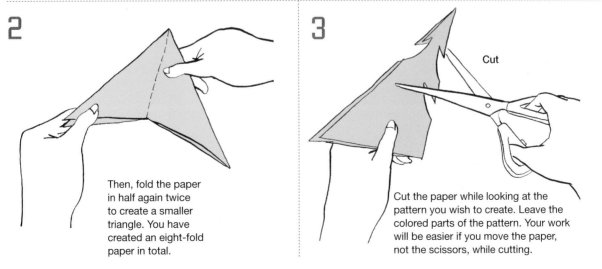

2

Then, fold the paper in half again twice to create a smaller triangle. You have created an eight-fold paper in total.

3 Cut

Cut the paper while looking at the pattern you wish to create. Leave the colored parts of the pattern. Your work will be easier if you move the paper, not the scissors, while cutting.

4

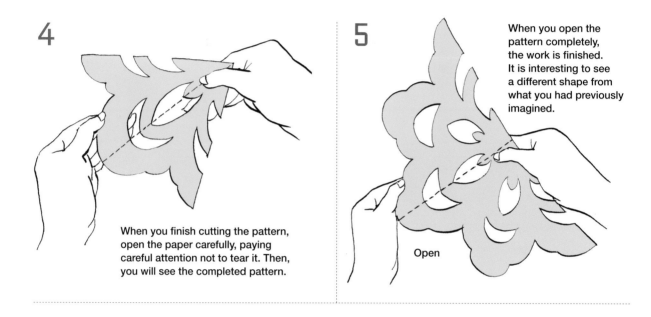

When you finish cutting the pattern, open the paper carefully, paying careful attention not to tear it. Then, you will see the completed pattern.

5

When you open the pattern completely, the work is finished. It is interesting to see a different shape from what you had previously imagined.

Open

Making a Triangle 1

Fold a square sheet of paper three or four times before cutting the pattern. This folding pattern is used for most of the paper stencils presented in this book.

Symbols	
	Valley fold (fold inward)–·–·–·–·–·–·–·–
	Mountain fold (fold outward)– – – – – – –
	Turn upside down

1

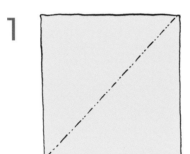

Fold a square in half.

2

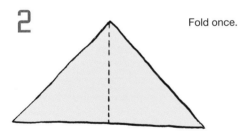

Fold once.

3

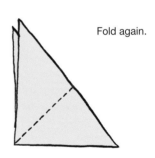

Fold again.

4

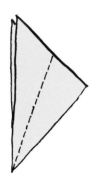

Fold for the third time.

STYLE △-01

POINT
For some designs, start cutting after this step.

5

Fold for the fourth time.

STYLE △-02

Making a Triangle 2

First, fold a square sheet of paper in half. Then, fold it twice at an angle of 60 degrees. Fold in half again before cutting the paper.

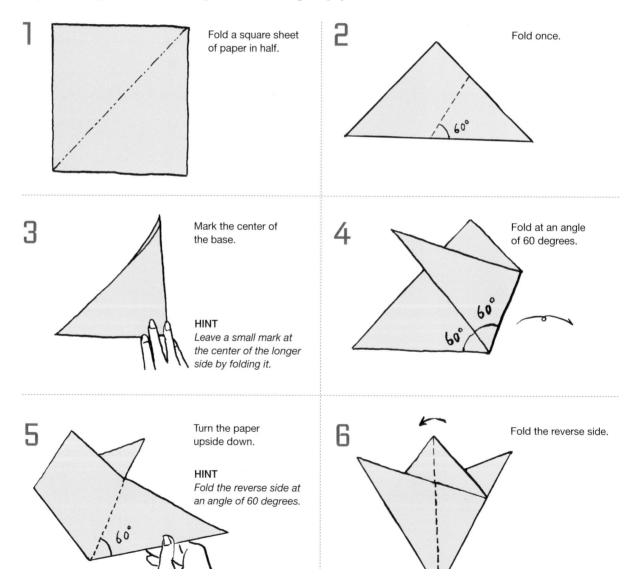

1 Fold a square sheet of paper in half.

2 Fold once.

3 Mark the center of the base.

HINT
Leave a small mark at the center of the longer side by folding it.

4 Fold at an angle of 60 degrees.

5 Turn the paper upside down.

HINT
Fold the reverse side at an angle of 60 degrees.

6 Fold the reverse side.

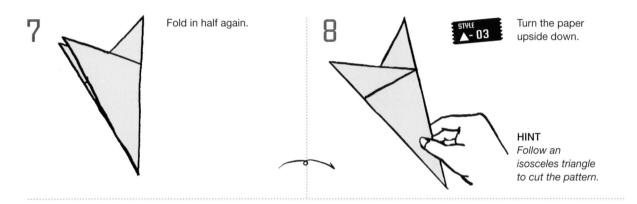

7 Fold in half again.

8 STYLE △-03   Turn the paper upside down.

HINT
Follow an isosceles triangle to cut the pattern.

Making a Rectangle

Fold a rectangular sheet of paper two or three times in the same direction to make a belt-like shape before cutting the pattern. You can create a different design from that of a triangle.

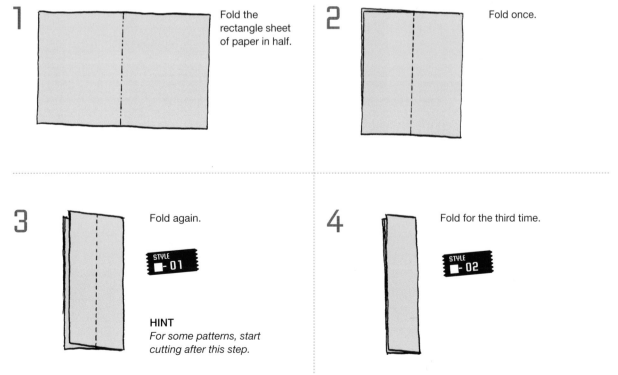

1 Fold the rectangle sheet of paper in half.

2 Fold once.

3 Fold again.

STYLE ☐-01

HINT
For some patterns, start cutting after this step.

4 Fold for the third time.

STYLE ☐-02

Packing for a New Trip
Basic Elements of Paper-Stencil Making

On the eve of my next trip, I pack my scissors, which I always carry with me during my travels, inside my suitcase. Then, I know that I am thoroughly prepared for another journey. But, I cannot sleep because of excitement. I open my travel guide while in bed. While reading through it, many different sceneries appear before my eyes. My heart starts to beat fast with anticipation. I calm myself by checking my luggage one more time. Still, the images do not stop popping up in my mind. What could be waiting for me in this next trip?

Pattern 3

Pattern 4

Pattern 5

Pattern 6

Kamakura, Japan

From afar, amidst the street lights, I see tiny summer flowers that point upward to the sky and make no sound. Occasionally, I notice something that I wasn't aware of before. The soft lights are lovely but melancholic, and they twinkle only for a split second in an ordinary night during an ordinary summer.

The noise of cicadas and the mugginess of the air are typical elements of a Japanese summer scene. I especially sense a nostalgic atmosphere in the small alleys of Kamakura that open to a breathtaking view of the peaceful ocean and the growing plants and trees.

I feel that I may have seen this scene sometime in my childhood.

I travelled leisurely around the city until evening came. I had my dinner early before visiting Tsurugaoka Hachiman Shrine. I didn't know why, but there were so many people around the area.

Then, I spotted a traditional Japanese theater that I had never seen before. It staged a performance with illuminations of many garden lanterns. I believe they hold this event every year. Colorful kimonos fluttered on the stage under fantastic lighting effects. I saw many tourists, and then I began to feel the hot air with a special sense of exaltation. I didn't want to leave the place, but I had to go back to the station. As I looked out through the train window, thinking that I hadn't seen fireworks yet that year, I noticed small fireworks from a distance. Certainly, you can get the best view of the lights and sounds of the fireworks from up close, but the scenery before me was something I only see once during summer. The small fireworks rose up to the night sky, then disappeared without sound. These images represent the peaceful and beautiful summer of Kamakura.

Pattern 1

This pattern is based on a design for a Japanese summer kimono (*yukata*) that symbolizes fireworks giving color to the night sky. First, cut small curves in the lower part of both sides of the paper, as though you were shaving them off. Cut from the upper left side to make a round shape, like overlapping two ovals, then cut a curve from the right side. To make a smooth curve, move the paper, and not the scissors.

Items of Inspiration

My friend gave me this lovely pottery as a gift. She chose it for me knowing my taste. I devote myself diligently to my creative work while thanking her for the daily chats and activities we shared tenderly together.

Pattern 2

Cut out a small slit by making two incisions near the center of the pattern on the right side of the paper. This will produce an acute angle that gives a strong impression to the pattern. On the left side of the paper, cut out a larger incision resembling a half petal. Finally, cut out the upper curve from both sides of the pattern as you did for Pattern 1.

STYLE
▲- 02

Pattern 3

On the longer, right side of the paper, cut out three half water drops in the same intervals from the center to the outer part of the entire pattern. Then, cut out the same two water drops on the other side. Place the water drops alternately on the right and left sides of the pattern in order to make it look attractive. Finally, cut off the outer part of the water drops that you cut previously.

Pattern 4

Cut out two half water drops on both sides of the paper near the center of the decoration, as you did for Pattern 3. Cut out smaller water drops right next to the first two. Then, cut around the rim of the water drops and make a deep, round incision. Do the same step on the other side of the pattern. Finally, cut off the outer part while tracing the rim. The outermost rim should be wider than the other lines to produce a well-balanced pattern.

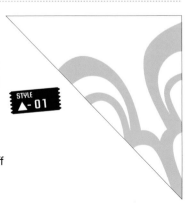

STYLE
▲-01

Pattern 5

Cut out two half water drops in the same size on each side of the paper. Then, cut along the outer rim of the water drops from the outer side of the decoration. Make a bud-shaped projection between the two water drops. If you make one projection smaller and the other one larger, the pattern will become beautiful.

STYLE ▲-01

Pattern 6

This pattern is a variation of Pattern 5. Cut out four half water drops in the same size on each side of the paper. If you use a larger piece of paper, you can make more water drops. Then, cut out the outer part of the pattern along the water drops. Make a bud-shaped projection on the dent of each side of the pattern. Change the positions and the number of buds to make variations.

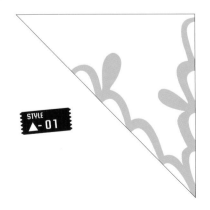

STYLE
▲-01

Pattern 1

Pattern 2

Pattern 3

Pattern 4

Pattern 5

Pattern 6

Pattern 7

Pattern 8

San Francisco, U.S.A.

The appetizing orange colors, brilliant strawberry-red market, light green plants blooming everywhere, colorful houses that shine under the sun—they all tell me something about the people's lives and their colorful surroundings.

A bus runs at night toward the center of the city. The moonlight is flickering on the surface of the water. I stayed for about a week at my friend's place; she was living in San Francisco as a foreign student. Although it was cold, I felt the warm wind having just arrived from London.

When I first visited this city, my friend instructed me to meet her at Union Square. I looked for the place on the map. I asked the bus driver for directions, but he asked me, "Where in Union Square?" I replied, "Take me anywhere in the square." It was a fine day and I spotted some benches around the square. I sat down while holding my suitcase on my lap. While waiting for my friend, I relaxed a bit with some coffee. I began to doze off and didn't know for how long I waited for my friend. Then, she arrived, and not having seen me for quite some time, smiled and walked toward me, calling my name. She looked more mature, and I was relieved to see her same charming face again, which hadn't changed since childhood. We went to see the ocean and crossed the bridge to eat some hamburgers. Then, we took the tram to visit some places until I felt my steps becoming lighter. I got so tired from the walk that I became sleepy. Whenever I talk with her in bed, I fall asleep before her.

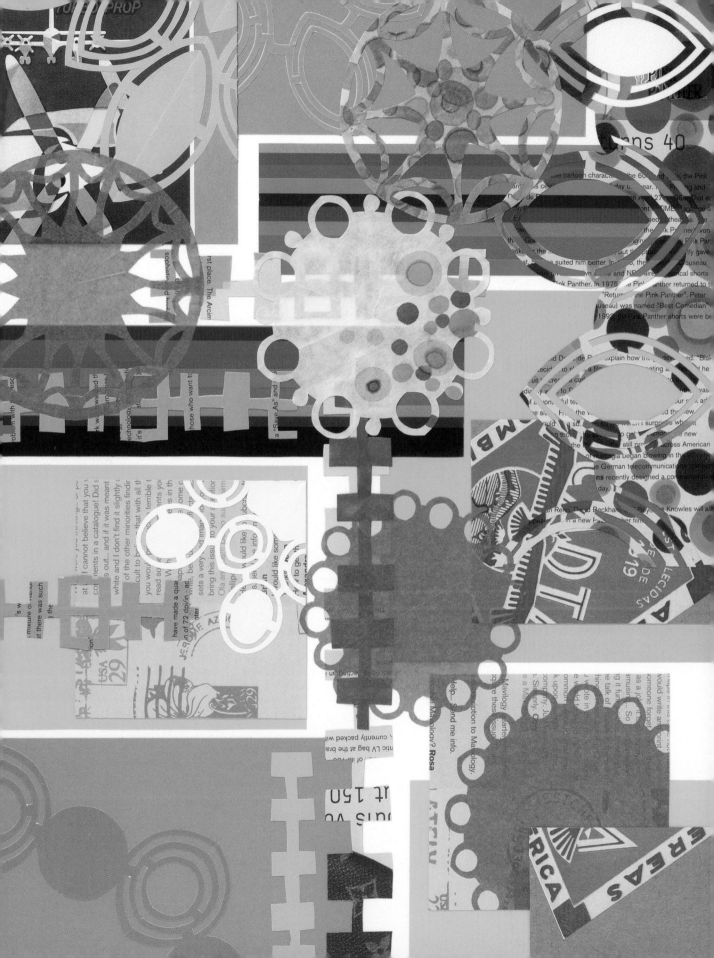

Pattern 1

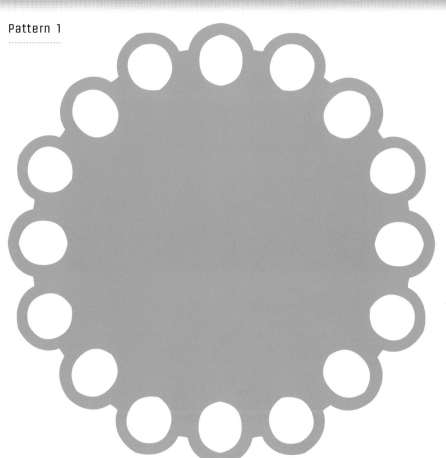

Cut out a half circle of the same distance from the center of each side of the paper. Cut off the unnecessary outer parts before cutting the circles in order to position them equidistant. Cut the outer part along the rim of the half circles to finish. If you cannot cut a perfect circle, it may mean that the angle from where you started to cut was too shallow.

Items of Inspiration

Sometimes, I easily fall in love with tableware at first sight. I especially love antique tableware. The light blue illustration on this bowl is incredibly attractive.

Pattern 2

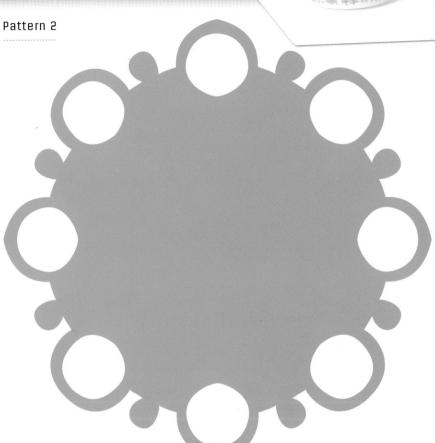

This pattern is a variation of Pattern 1. Make an isosceles triangle by cutting off the outer side of the paper in order to produce perfect circles easily. Cut out a half circle on each side, then cut off the outer portion along the circles. Cut a bump between the circles.

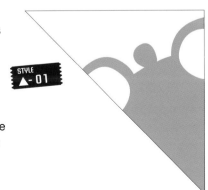

STYLE
▲-01

Pattern 3

Cut off the outer portion of the paper to make a perfect circle when you open it. Cut the inner side of the circle along the curve that you first made from both sides, making sure to leave the middle part. Then, cut toward the slit that you have made from the lower part of the pattern. Finally, cut out triangular shapes at the bottom, making natural curves on both sides. Maintain the constant width for the circular frame to make a perfect circle.

STYLE
▲-01

Pattern 4

This pattern is a variation of Pattern 3. Fold the paper again before starting to cut. First, cut off the outer portion of the paper to make a circle, as you did in Pattern 3. Cut the paper along the curve of the circle from both sides, then cut off the incisions. Finally, cut out a triangle on the left side, making natural curves, then do the same step on the right side of the pattern.

STYLE ▲ - 02

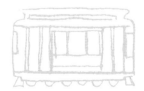

Pattern 5

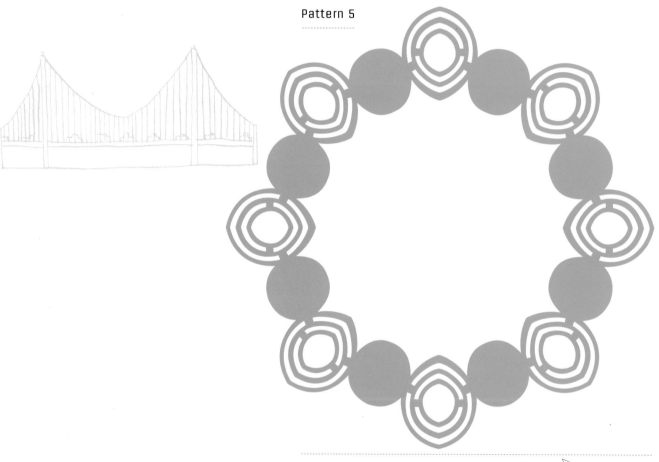

First, cut out a small half circle on the right side of the paper. Cut out the curves around the half circle from both ends. Make two curved cut-outs while placing the connected parts in different locations to make an attractive design. Cut the rim of the circle along the curves. Finally, cut out the outer portion while leaving a half circle on the left side.

STYLE
▲- 02

Pattern 6

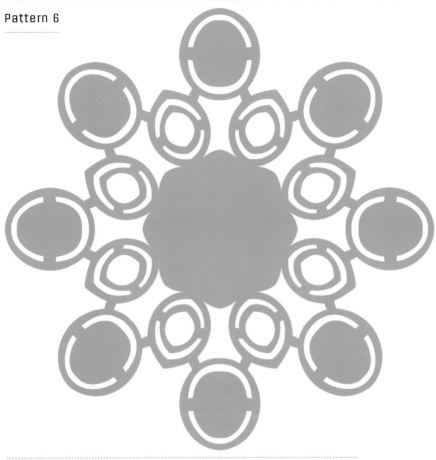

First, cut out a small half circle on the left side. Cut out curves around the circle from both ends. On the right side, cut out two curved lines around the circle. Cut off the outer portion along the circles to finish. Be careful not to cut off the connected parts. Try to make beautiful curves for the circles in order to produce an attractive design.

STYLE
▲- 02

Pattern 7

This pattern can be made by stretching the circles in Pattern 6. First, cut out a long half circle on the left side of the paper, then make two curved lines along the circle. On the right side, cut out only the curved lines to make it the outline of a long half circle. Then, cut off the outer portion along the shapes you have just cut out. Finally, cut the paper, leaving a half circle near the center of the pattern.

STYLE ▲- 02

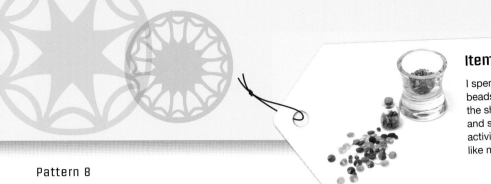

Pattern 8

Prepare a square piece of paper, then cut out an image of stretched circles that were made in Pattern 7. Cut out a long half circle on the right side of the paper. Then, make several curved lines along the circle. Do the same step for the left side, cutting out the same half circle, but placing it a bit lower than the right one in order to make a pattern. Finally, cut off the outer portion along the two half circles.

STYLE
▲-01

Pattern 1

Pattern 2

Pattern 3

Pattern 4

Pattern 5

Pattern 6

Pattern 7

Pattern 8

Montego Bay, Jamaica

The rich greens amidst colorful flowers, vast sky, and shiny water, and the sweet fragrance of fruits—I relax my shoulders while listening to the soft sound of the melting ice. I walk slowly where the wind guides me, then I stretch my body and sleep. I will remember this scene forever.

How many hours did I spend on the plane since I left Japan in early spring? I had to make two stopovers in North American cities before reaching my destination. I hadn't had such a long air travel experience for quite some time. I thought it might have been too much to travel this far from the everyday bustle of Japan, but as soon as I arrived in Jamaica for the first time in my life, I walked briskly through the concourse of the crowded airport. Outside the airport, a dense blanket of green caught my eyes as the sky started to dim. The plants swayed with the strong wind. I felt the comfortable daylight heat touch my skin.

I got in a car to proceed to the hotel while listening to Bob Marley's music. (I don't know if his music is only played for tourists.) Since it was already late, there weren't many places that served dinner, so I stopped by at a local fast-food restaurant. It had a murky look, and the car stopped right in front of it. I approached the dark restaurant. It was smoky inside, and I saw that they were roasting chicken on direct fire in the grill. I got excited to see such a "wild" way of cooking for the first time in my life. The smell of the roasted chicken was exotic and familiar to me. I chose this destination because I wanted to see the Caribbean Sea. I realized I did not need any other reason to visit this place when I saw the beautiful scenery from my window and felt the breeze in the early morning. Throughout my stay, I napped and had fruit drinks, walked, and went horseback riding, always surrounded by wild flowers, and the transparent sky and sea. Ironically, I thought that I shouldn't experience such a wonderful trip with its tender and sweet fragrance because the moments were probably too sweet for me.

Pattern 1

Cut out an image of branches or leaves growing from the trees on the tropical island of Jamaica. Cut from the left side of the paper, and form images of long and thin leaves. Try to create natural curves that look like actual leaves. Make each leaf thin and its tips sharp in order to produce attractive leaves.

STYLE
▲- 01

Items of Inspiration

The days I spent relaxing on the beach were special moments. I almost lost my materialistic instinct, but as soon as I entered a souvenir shop, I was attracted to the variety of display items.

Pattern 2

This pattern is a variation of Pattern 1. In order to make a circular pattern, cut out the outer side in a round shape after folding the paper. Do not make pointed tips with this pattern. Cut out a thick and short stem on the left side, then cut out three thinner stems along the first one. Finally, cut out a shorter stem on the right side to finish.

STYLE △-01

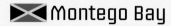
Pattern 3

This pattern is a variation of Pattern 2. First, cut out a short stem, then cut out two more stems that bend toward the first one. Cut out a short and thick stem on the right side, then a thinner one that bends toward the right one. This pattern is similar to the previous ones wherein the stems extend from the center to the outer side, except that you have to change the length and directions of each stem. Be creative to make different designs.

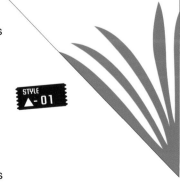

STYLE
▲-01

Pattern 4

Cut out the stem on the left side of the paper. Cut the paper in a long L shape and turn back the scissors to make a long and oval shape. Then, cut a rectangle right next to it. Next, cut out the stems to make them look like they stick out of the oval shape. Do the same step on the right side and cut out a long rectangle to finish.

STYLE
▲- 01

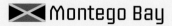

Pattern 5

Cut the paper while forming two points at the center of the pattern. Cut out three small triangles from the upper right side, toward one of the cores, then cut out the rest of the parts around it. Do the same step on the left side and cut out small triangles. Now, the pattern looks like lines that gather together at the core. Finally, make a similar pattern with the other core on the lower side.

Items of Inspiration

A basket vendor with dreadlocks was sitting lazily in front of his baskets of various sizes, at a corner of the hotel. He was always waiting for a customer to come by. He talked to me each time I passed by so finally, I bought one basket on the last day of my visit.

Pattern 6

This pattern is a variation of Pattern 5. Cut out the lines carefully having the same image of lines spreading out from the cores. Cut out a few triangles in order to determine the positions of the cores, then cut out a connecting line to the cores. You can also make some short lines for accent.

Pattern 7

Cut out a piece of paper in the form of an image of waves. First, cut out a gradual curve from the right side of the paper to show an image of high and low waves. Turn back the scissors in the center to cut out a wavy slit. Then, cut out another slit from the other side to make it look like it continues from the wave on the right side. Make two more wavy slits below the first one, then finally, cut off the upper portion. The connected parts in the waves should be placed in different positions.

Pattern 8

First, cut out the uppermost wide curve. It is the same pattern as Pattern 7, except for the width of the waves. Cut out waves from both sides, making smooth S shapes. Finally, cut off the upper and lower parts of the pattern with the same curve. You can also make your own wave design.

STYLE
▲-01

Pattern 1

Pattern 2

Prague, Czech Republic

The city of Prague is enveloped by unique shadows, and the noise of the city flows with the clear breeze. The ordinary sound of the bell seems new to me. All day long I can hear someone playing beautiful tunes from afar. These scenes inspire me to create paper stencils as a gesture of my respect for the writers and artists of this city.

I made the decision to go to Prague without much thinking or information about the city. The name "Prague" had a beautiful sound to my ears, and true enough, the city turned out to be immensely beautiful and more lively than I had imagined.

More than ten years ago, the country became an independent nation. The local people welcomed us very warmheartedly. The first thing I recall about this place is the memory of going to a classical concert. The ticket was surprisingly affordable, and I was amazed by the magnificent and fine decorations of the concert hall. When the concert finally began, I heard the sound, "ting!" The lingering sound remained in the hall for a long time. When it faded, the sound repeated—"ting!"—then, there was another long reverberation. All of a sudden, the sound connected to my childhood memory and I started to shake my shoulders while holding back my laughter. My giggle was so infectious that the person right next to me started to laugh as well while holding back his voice. I had a hard time holding back my laughter. The huge orchestra remained silent for some time. I enjoyed that wonderful moment and the music after my laughter had stopped. After the concert, I went to a restaurant that was recommended to me. I talked and laughed about the previous scene with my friend. That funny and enjoyable memory comes back to me whenever I visit a concert hall.

Pattern 3

Pattern 4

Pattern 1

This pattern has an image of an iron fence or a bridge railing with elegant curves, which I spotted in Prague. First, start by cutting a curve from the upper right side, then make a small circle at the center, then go back along the first half of the curve. On the left side of the pattern, make a similar but larger pattern. Finally, cut off the surroundings along the two round shapes.

Pattern 2

First, cut out a curve from the upper left side of the paper, and make a small circle. Make a similar pattern at the lower right side. Then, cut out the square part on the left side around the two shapes you just cut out. Cut out the large and small crescent shapes on the right side. Finally, cut out the surroundings with smooth curves to finish.

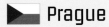

Pattern 3

The basic image of this design is two long and thin leaves connected vertically on the left of the paper. First, cut out a long half circle on the upper left side of the paper. Do the same step for the lower leaf, but make two branches as an accent. Then, extend the branches from the joints made on the left side toward the right side. To finish, make the swirl decoration on the top leaf.

 STYLE ▲-02

Pattern 4

Cut out smooth curves, crossing each other, that resemble Pattern 3. Begin with the decoration on the top side, then cut from the left side. After making a small circle on the tip, go back toward the center of the design, then change the angle to cut it off toward the right side. On the right side, cut out three portions while imagining a large and long leaf. Cut out the left side parts along the large leaf to finish.

Pattern 1

Pattern 2

Berlin, Germany

The city of Berlin gives a distinct impression on any day, whether clear or cloudy. The old buildings stand quietly with a solid and grave appearance. Every morning I would go to a comfortable café, and visit the elegant restaurant that I discovered. I tried to relive my life in various ways in this city.

This was my third visit to Berlin. I did not expect that I would become so familiar with this city. Everyone says that Berlin has a unique atmosphere due to its elaborate historical background. Since the winter season is long in this country, spring is a better season to enjoy the city. People take out chairs in the parks, and beer gardens open in May. People chat and enjoy drinking beer while munching on large frankfurters in their bread. Germans are big but they look somehow bigger than they actually are. We can eat seasonal vegetables in restaurants, and I frequently saw white asparagus while I was there. I never had white asparagus before until I went to Germany. Since then, it has become my favorite vegetable. I looked for it in the menu everyday when I had dinner.

Since my second visit, I had been under some pressure, unlike my usual travels, because I was in Berlin for my exhibition. I had more chances to talk with people and spend time thinking about my future plans. It was a good opportunity for me to take a look at my own works objectively in a place different from my usual exhibition destinations. I treasured that moment. On a rainy day, I spent my lunch time relaxing alone and enjoyed reading books among the company of regular customers. I tend to be pressured by work, and feel I have to do something at home. My stay in Berlin offered me precious moments to think about some things while looking at unfamiliar landscapes and listening to the gentle sound of raindrops.

Pattern 3

Pattern 4

Pattern 1

I made some reproductions of German cityscapes through paper stencils. One is an image of church steeples. First, cut out a small triangle on the right side of the paper. Then, cut out a wide and straight line along the triangle's leg. Next, cut out a roof shape around it, continuing toward another smaller triangular spire on the left side. The secret in forming good shapes is to align the bases of the triangles horizontally.

Items of Inspiration

Flea markets abound on a relaxing weekend in Europe. They are always crowded with lots of people. As I rambled through the alleys, I picked up something and put it back, then I started walking again. Then, I found this compass, which had a strange color and shape.

Pattern 2

This pattern shows an image of triangle spires that stick out to the upper and lower sides of the paper. First, cut out a triangle on the upper-right side and a line right below it. Then, on the other side, cut out a triangle and a line underneath, and cut out another triangle under the line. Cut off the outer parts along the roof shapes. Finally, cut out a small triangle on the lower-right side to finish.

STYLE
▲ - 02

Pattern 3

This pattern shows an image of round domes. First, make the bigger dome on the right side of the paper. Cut out the first curve closest to the center of the dome. Then, cut out other curves along the first dome, from the center to the outside. The finished image of the building is better if you align the base of the curves at the same level. On the other side, make a similar dome, then finally, cut off the outer part.

Pattern 4

First, cut out several half circles in different sizes on each side of the square. Cut out the spaces between the circles to make the entire design look like it is connected with curved lines. Keep the width of the lines constant and try to make smooth curves so that the pattern will look beautiful.

STYLE ▲-01

Pattern 1

Pattern 2

Pattern 3

Pattern 4

Pattern 5

Pattern 6

Vienna, Austria

The snowfall has finally stopped after it snowed all night. Now, where do I go? As soon as I leave, my footsteps on the thin-layered white-covered street, I do not stop walking. Then, I stop for a while in front of some drawings that I remember seeing in some books. I cut out my own shapes from a piece of paper, keeping them as tokens of my memories.

After changing trains several times from one city to another, I finally arrived in Vienna. It was a lot colder than the other cities I had visited. As I imagined, when I saw the garden of the guesthouse in the morning, for the first time since I arrived, the landscape was covered with snow from the previous night. I get excited whenever I see a snow scene, and this reaction has not changed since my childhood.

We rushed out to the garden, but we got tired since it was almost the end of our trip. Travelling with friends is fun; we can look after each other and express our joy when we see the sights. I don't like to be alone. However, that moment was different. Three of us wanted to be alone, so we went separate ways that day.

First, I opened a travel guide and decided to ride the ferris wheel, for no reason. The old ferris wheel had many small capsules and moved around quietly. As it was early morning, I was the only one in the capsule for eight people. The capsule had a heater, so it felt slightly warm inside. While looking over the entire city, I heard myself say, "Wow, it's beautiful!", then, I visited three museums. By the time I arrived at the third museum, it was getting dark. At the entrance, I saw two familiar figures who were my friends. Each of us planned to visit the last museum at the end of the day, but I learned that we went to almost the same places after all. Afterwards, we talked about dinner and restarted our travel together.

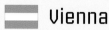
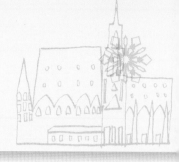

Pattern 1

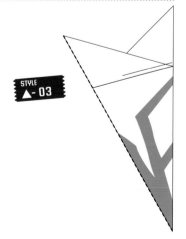

This pattern shows an image of falling snow from the Vienna skies. Unlike the previous patterns, this pattern starts with a triangle of an angle of 30 degrees. For the first pattern, cut from the right side of the paper. Cut out a triangle and a rectangle that resembles a half-shaped large sword. Cut off the outer part along the sword, then make a smaller sword on the left side.

Items of Inspiration

The reindeer designs on small items give some modest impression that girls like very much. My boyfriend, who is a lot more romantic than I am, selected gifts with such gentle colors.

Pattern 2

This pattern shows an image of flowerlike snowflakes. The design on the tip is fine and distinctive. First, cut out a small triangle near the center of the paper. Pay attention to the angles of the triangle in order to make a starlike shape when the pattern is opened. Then, cut out a near-triangle and another triangle. Finally, cut out the outer part, which looks like several bars sticking out.

STYLE ▲- 03

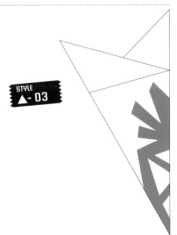

Pattern 3

This pattern is a variation of Pattern 2. You can change the fine designs of the central motif and its surroundings. First, cut off the center of the paper, diagonally. When the paper is opened, it forms a starlike shape with six arms. Then, cut out a small rectangle on the left side of the pattern. Cut off the outer part that has three projections, finally, move the scissors upward through the right side to cut.

STYLE ▲- 03

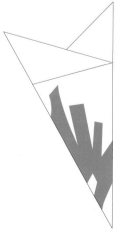

Pattern 4

First, cut out a sharp-angled triangle at the center of the paper. This part will form a star with twelve points. Cut out another triangle near the center on the left side, then a rectangle positioned slightly above the triangle. On the right side of the pattern, make an image of a thin sword. Cut off the outer part along the images that you made previously, making a small triangle projection on the left side of the pattern.

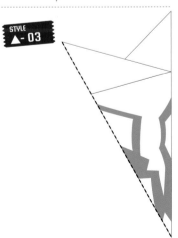

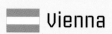 
Pattern 5

This pattern is made by adding some curves to the previous patterns. First, cut out a triangle with curves on the left side of the paper. On the right side of the triangle, cut out a rectangle and a small triangle. Then, cut out the outer part from the left side while making a small sword shape on the upper right side. Finally, make a small triangle on the tip of the sword.

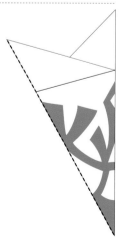

Pattern 6

Make six bud shapes for this pattern by first cutting out the bud design shown here. Cut out a triangle with curves around the center of the left side of the paper. Cut out the insides of the bud, then cut off the center in a V shape. Finally, cut out the rest of the pattern while paying attention to the bud shapes.

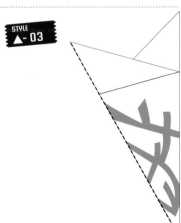

Decorating Your Travel Memories
with Paper Stencils

When I open my suitcase, which is loaded with so many travel memories, I smell the cities that I have visited, and suddenly begin to miss them. Museum and theater brochures, bus and train tickets, wrapping paper from charming shops—all of these items become precious souvenirs from my travels. Make your own paper-stencil designs based on your travels before your memories fade.

Japanese Paper Bowl

Make a bowl-like shape with paper layers. The paper flowers bloom on the table.

Tear a piece of paper into several pieces and stick them on a bowl using glue. The firmly layered paper produces a beautiful paper plate. Put your snacks or small articles in it and enjoy your decorative paper stencils.

Materials

Paper stencil patterns
Aluminum foil
Washi (Japanese paper)
  in two colors
Bowl (for molding)
Liquid glue
Brush

1
Cut some aluminum foil about 1½ times larger than the bowl.

2
Cover the bowl with the foil and press it onto the bowl to make a bowl-like shape.

3
Tear some washi paper (purple paper in the photo) into 2-inch (5 cm) squares.

4
Stick the washi on the aluminum foil with liquid glue.

5
Tear some white washi as you did in Step 3, and stick them over the first washi paper that you used.

6
Remove the molded foil from the bowl, then stick washi on the other side of the foil.

7
When the entire bowl is covered with colored paper, stick a paper stencil on the bottom of the bowl.

8
Finally, stick a paper stencil pattern inside the bowl.

Mobiles

Mobiles sway and turn against the flow of the wind. They remind me of my travels each time I look at them.

When I hang this mobile in my room, I recall my past memories of the city I visited, as though I can feel the same wind from that time blowing amidst the bright sunshine.

Materials

Paper stencil patterns
Cardboard (for mounting)
Lace
Beads
Glue
Compass
Scissors
Awl
Double-sided tape

1  Select three paper stencil patterns of the same size, and stick them on the cardboard with glue.

2  Draw a circle around the paper stencils with a compass, leaving some margin around them.

3  Cut out the stencils carefully with scissors along the circles that you have just drawn.

4  Turn the stencils upside down, and mark a line with an awl through the center to divide them in half.

5  Turn the stencils upright again, and fold them inward along the mark.

6 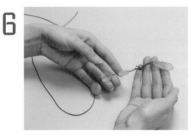 Pass a string of waxed lace through some beads. Make several knots to hold the beads and the paper stencils.

7  Paste the two stencils that were folded in half together with glue, as shown at the left.

8  Grasp the lace with the center of the three pasted stencils, and stick them together with double-sided tape to finish.

 Montego Bay,
Jamaica

Scrapbook

Transfer your travel
memories into bright
colors and different
kinds of paper to
make your own book.

Materials

Paper stencil patterns
Cardboard (for the
    book cover)
Colored paper (for
    the endpaper)
Newspaper
Thread
Needle
Awl
Double-sided tape
Paper clip
Ruler

A = Two sheets of cardboard for the book cover (cardboard in C size + bundle for the book spine)
B = Two sheets of cardboard for the endpaper (cardboard in C size x 2 + bundle for the book spine)
C = Paper for the text pages (e.g., newspaper, as shown above)
Cut the paper into an appropriate size and make a bundle with it.

1 Put the two sheets of material A together using double-sided tape, overlapping them slightly to make the spine.

2 Turn the cardboard upside down and paste on some paper stencils with spray glue.

3 Overlap two sheets of material B together, and clip them with bundle C. Then, stick it on the wrong side of the spine of material A using double-sided tape.

4 Place the ruler about ½ inch (1.2 cm) inside the sewn end of the book, and make holes with an awl at intervals of ⅘ inch (2 cm).

5 Pass a piece of thread through the needle and through the holes on the book vertically and horizontally several times.

6 Repeat Step 5 until the book spine is sewn in T shapes, as shown at the left.

7 Finally, put the upright side of B and the back of A together with double-sided tape to finish.

Prague,
Czech Republic

Powder Stencil

Store your travel
memories in a
stencil pattern,
and taste the cake
while talking about
your travels with
your friend. Help
yourself to more
bites by sprinkling
your memories in
a cute pattern over
the cake.

Materials

Paper stencil patterns
Stencil sheet
Cake (appropriate size
 for the stencils, such as
 a simple chocolate cake)
Powder (powdered sugar,
 cocoa powder, etc.
 Consider the color
 contrast with the cake.)
Sieve
Cutting knife
Cutting mat

1

Affix a stencil sheet over the paper stencil, and cut out the pattern with a craft knife.

2

Place the stencil sheet that you just carved over the cake.

3

Sprinkle powdered sugar over the cake evenly using a sieve.

4

When the cake's surface is covered completely with the powder, remove the stencil sheet gently.

Planter
Base

Try to enhance
the image of
Germany with
a soft streamline.

Materials

Plastic sheet
Plastic bolts and nuts
Awl
Ruler
Hole puncher
Scissors

1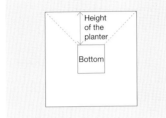

Fold the plastic sheet on the dotted lines. Cut the sheet to the size of the planter.

2

Carve the lines to be folded with an awl using a ruler.

3

Fold the plastic sheet with your hands along the carved lines.

4

Make holes about 3 to 3½ inches (8 to 9 cm) from each corner using a hole puncher.

5

Place plastic bolts into the holes and put all four corners together with nuts.

6

Cut the designs on the corner. (The design to the left features Berlin Pattern 1. See page 68.)

7

Repeat for the rest of the corners.

8

If you open the design on the corners as an accent, the planter base will have a different impression.

**Vienna,
Austria**

Wrapping
Cloth

I wrapped a gift
containing my
special memories for
an important person.

 Materials

Paper stencil patterns
Wrapping cloth (*furoshiki*)
Stencil sheet
Stencil brush
Paint for cloth
Craft knife
Cutting mat

1  Affix a stencil sheet over the paper stencil, and cut out the pattern.

2  Place the pattern on the wrapping cloth and color it with paint while tapping the stencil brush.

3  When the pattern is dyed thoroughly, remove the stencil gently.

4  Finally, repeat the previous steps with different stencils and colors.

Afterword: Climax of My Travels

While I was working on this book, I made a trip
to a city that I had never visited before in my life.
I had to rush a project and clean my house until
the last minute on the day before departure.
On my way to that city, I could feel and picture the
wind, sound, smell, colors, and many other images
of that city in my mind. I know these images would
assist me in finding clues for developing my daily
creative work.

Unfortunately, every trip has its end. When that
moment arrives, I always become emotional
while looking back at my trip and thinking about
tomorrow. I would remember the pleasant
tiredness I felt after a long walk, or the new
encounter with someone, and the various other
events that took place.

I am so grateful for all those days that gave me
a sense of fulfillment and the opportunity to learn
more about the art of decorative paper stencils.

I would like to show my appreciation to
everyone who has discovered this book and to
those who always support my work. I hope to
continue enhancing my creative endeavors to be
able to discover my original design.

About the Author: Kanako Yaguchi

Born in 1976, Kanako graduated from the Department of Design at Joshibi University of Art and Design, Japan. As a student, she held an exhibition, entitled "Yorokobinokatachi" ("Shapes of Pleasure") and started activities for inventing various shapes of decorative paper stencils, or "kirigami." Her personal artwork is full of new discoveries and expressions of the good old days, which have fascinated people around the world. Her current job involves holding individual exhibitions while collaborating with the apparel industry. She also does store and logo design and holds workshops based on decorative paper stencils. Her work has been introduced in various media. Recently, she has been actively involved with projects in other countries, which widen the scope of her artistic work and expression. Kanako's aim is to discover the further creative potential of paper-stencil making as reflected in her works. Her other publications include *The Art of Decorative Paper Stencils* (Quarry Books) and *The Book of Decorative Paper Stencils for Adults* (PHP Institute, available only in Japanese).

Appendix: Making Stencils With New Paper to Relive Travel Memories

While recalling my travel memories of the various cities I have visited, I created different types of new paper samples using a variety of colors and patterns. I hope to create more designs that will invoke different impressions about my travels. I hope you can also experience wonderful encounters in your own trips.

The attached paper samples can also be used as wrapping paper as they are thinner and crisper than the samples in the previous edition. Choose your favorite paper and cut it along the dotted line to detach it from the book. Then, cut it into a square or a rectangle of your desired size to create a stencil pattern.

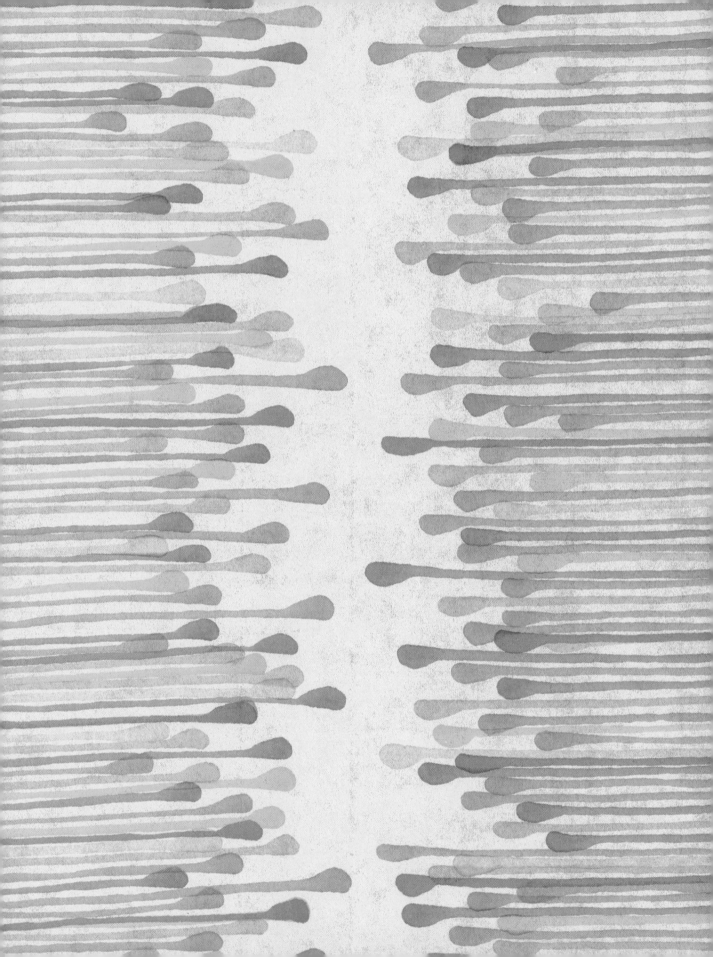

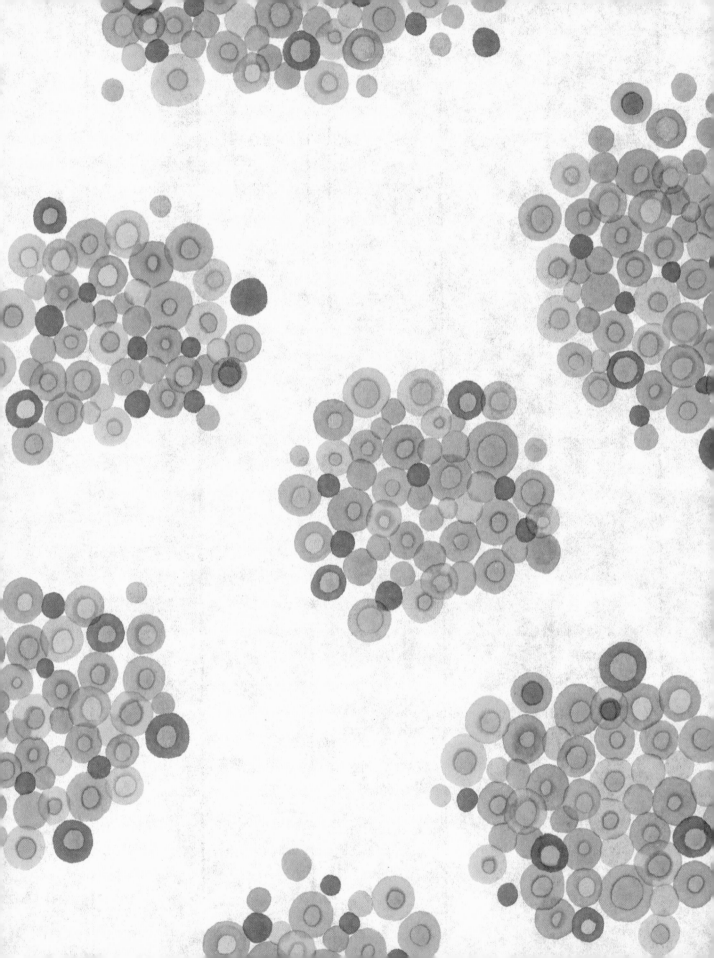